INSIDE OUT

CONNECTING WORD TO LIFE

Bible Society
Stonehill Green
Westlea
Swindon SN5 7DG
biblesociety.org.uk

First published by The Salvation Army under the title *Shelf Life*.
Revised and updated edition published 2020 by The Salvation Army and Bible Society.

ISBN: 978-0-564-04907-3

Design and production by Bible Society Resources Ltd, a wholly owned subsidiary of The British and Foreign Bible Society.

BSRL/7.05M/2020
Printed in Great Britain

Founded by William and Catherine Booth in 1865, **The Salvation Army** is active in more than 130 countries offering God's hope and love to all those in need without discrimination. The calling to fight against social injustice among society's most vulnerable and marginalised – to encourage both social and spiritual transformation – is central to the mission of The Salvation Army. To find out more about who we are, including our work with young people, visit our website at salvationarmy.org.uk or social media @youthchildrensa

Across the world, millions of people are not able to engage with the Bible. This is often because the Scriptures aren't available or accessible, or because their significance and value haven't yet been recognised. Working in over 200 countries, **Bible Society** is a charity and on a global mission to offer the Bible to every man, woman and child. This is because we believe that when people engage with the Bible, lives can be changed, for good.

CONTENTS

This is your Bible discovery guide to help you get your Bible off your shelf and into your life!

WELCOME TO

INSIDE OUT

Connecting word to life

CONTAINED WITHIN THIS GUIDE YOU WILL FIND

 facts about the most amazing book that ever was ... and still is!

 clear info about resources that will specifically help you, as a young person, connect with the Bible in a relevant, fresh way.

 tips on how to read between the lines, get inside the story of the Bible and live out its meaning in our lives.

 ideas to bring the words to life and enable you to meet with God.

 six 'Connectives' to guide your Bible reading experience and steps into action.

 suggestions for ways of studying the Bible on your own or with a group.

SOPHIE

'It's taught me the best way to treat people. It makes me want to be a better person to the people that I care about.'

NATHAN

'I've seen lots of verses about not to worry and giving your cares to God, and since then I've worried a lot less.'

CHLOE

'Once you get into the routine of reading a Bible, good stuff will come from it!'

BEN

'By reading the Bible I've been inspired, and I've lived that out in my life every day.'

OLGA

'I love reading the Bible because it has personal anecdotes about people's encounters with God.'

SAM

'Where Jesus commands people to be healed, it's just so powerful, and I think the power of the name of Jesus is just amazing.'

You can see these and other quotes from young people by watching a video at gnbyouthedition.co.uk/stories

The Bible is one of the most influential documents in the whole of history and has been transforming people's lives for thousands of years.

Great leaders of the past, such as American civil rights activist Dr Martin Luther King, have been inspired by its teachings. Even though it was written so long ago, it's still relevant to our lives right here, right now. The Bible is God's living word – it's what God wants to say to us now and in the future. Through the words in the Bible, God tells us about who we are, who he wants us to become, his dreams for his world and his love for his people. The words are inspiring, exciting, challenging, informing and comforting.

Reading the Bible is not simply reading, it's getting together with God!

The Bible has something to say about almost all the questions we might be asking – whether about our relationships, our purpose here on earth or how to live a good life. People in really tough situations have read the Bible and found themselves changed. God speaks to us through the Bible, bringing a message of hope, love, forgiveness, freedom and purpose.

We learn that nothing can ever separate us from God's love, and we find out more about this God who loves us unconditionally and can make a difference to us today.

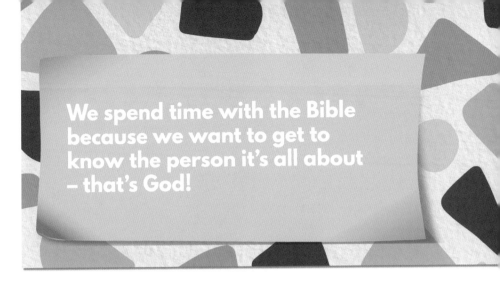

We spend time with the Bible because we want to get to know the person it's all about – that's God!

The BiBLe is the StoRY OF GOD, PAST, PReSeNt AND FUTURe.

We will soon discover that God speaks to us clearly and personally through the Bible. God will not love us more because we read the Bible, or reject us if we don't. However, getting into the Bible means getting to know God. We can grow in our faith and learn to become more like Jesus.

GETTING STARTED

Through reading the Bible, we see that there is far more to the world, more to us, more to what we see and more to what we don't see – more to everything! – than we had ever dreamed, and that this 'more' has to do with God. As we read, and the longer we read, we begin to 'get it' – we are in conversation with God. We find ourselves listening and answering in matters that most concern us: who we are, where we came from, where we are going, what makes us tick, the texture of the world and the communities we live in, and – most of all – the incredible love of God among us, doing for us what we cannot do for ourselves.

Eugene Peterson:
Introduction to *THE MESSAGE*

1.
Find a time when you can read the Bible on a regular basis.

2.
Find a space where you are comfortable and can concentrate.

3.
Get your Bible, a pen or a pencil and a notebook or journal.

4.
Ask God to help you understand what you read.

5.
Read the Bible passage.

6.
Think and pray about what you have learned.

7.
Jot down any insights, prayers or actions to take in your journal.

So, first things first, have you got a Bible? We don't mean any old Bible; we mean a Bible that is specifically yours. (It is probably best to avoid digging out an old Bible from your grandparents' garage, blowing the dust off the creased-up pages and reading with the musty smell of damp in your nostrils!) Your choice of Bible is vitally important and full of meaning; many people discover that the first ever Bible they choose for themselves stays with them well into their adulthood. It becomes a familiar and trusted companion on their journey as a follower of Jesus.

A great choice to start with would be Bible Society's Good News Bible Youth Edition, which has interesting facts, challenges and creative journalling activities to bring the words on the pages to life.

Go to gnbyouthedition.co.uk for more info and to find links to **30 YouTube videos** that accompany the Bible.

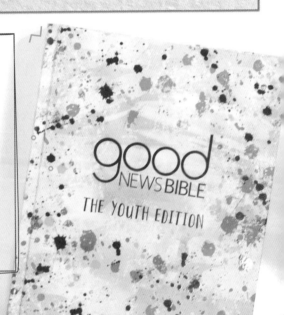

WHAT DO YOU LOOK FOR IN A BIBLE?

If you decide the GNB Youth Edition isn't for you, the first thing you must consider when choosing a Bible is which translation you prefer. The Bible was originally written in Hebrew, Aramaic and Greek, and there are many different English translations available.

Some aim to be word-for-word translations, such as the New King James Version (NKJV) or the New Revised Standard Version (NRSV). These generally use more traditional Bible language.

Other versions translate the meaning of the text into a more modern style of language and are easier to understand. One example is the New International Version (NIV). Other translations are written as a paraphrase of the text, such as *The Message*. These bring the Scriptures to life in a way relevant for today.

HERE'S MATTHEW 5.13 IN FOUR DIFFERENT BIBLE TRANSLATIONS

'You are the salt of the earth; but if the salt loses its flavour, how shall it be seasoned?'

MATTHEW 5.13 (NKJV)

'You are the salt of the earth. But if the salt loses its saltiness, how can it be made salty again?'

MATTHEW 5.13 (NIV)

'You are the salt of the earth; but if salt has lost its taste, how can its saltiness be restored?'

MATTHEW 5.13 (NRSV)

'Let me tell you why you are here. You're here to be salt-seasoning that brings out the God-flavours of this earth. If you lose your saltiness, how will people taste godliness?'

MATTHEW 5.13 (MSG)

ABOUT THE BIBLE

The shortest verse in the English Bible is only two words: Jesus wept.

JOHN 11.35

The longest psalm in the Bible is Psalm 119: it has 176 verses.

The Bible is, in fact, not just one book but a large collection of books by around 40 different authors.

THE BIBLE CONTAINS STORIES, HISTORY LESSONS, LAWS, POEMS, LETTERS, PROPHECIES AND MUCH MORE.

At least 1.5 billion people have no access to a full Bible translation in their first language.[1]

The Bible is the bestselling book of all time.

The Bible as we have it, in its current form, is basically about 2,000 years old, but the Old Testament is much older.

In some countries of the world, such as North Korea, owning a Bible or religious literature is very dangerous and could result in imprisonment or even death.

OVER 3,000 LANGUAGES HAVE AT LEAST PART OF THE BIBLE IN TRANSLATION.[2]

1 wycliffe.org.uk/about/our-story
2 wycliffe.org.uk/about/our-impact

To find out more about how the Bible came together, such as when and how the books of the New Testament were chosen, watch a short video at gnbyouthedition.co.uk/bibletogether.

REASONS MY BIBLE STAYS ON THE SHELF!

I don't understand it!

How do I know it's true?

I just don't have the time!

It seems irrelevant to my life!

I find it boring!

The Bible says things I don't like!

It's so big, I don't know where to start!

Other people will think I'm weird if I read the Bible!

ADD YOUR OWN REASONS HERE

Hmmm ... there's a lot of excuses we give for not reading the Bible.
Let's examine them in more detail.

I don't understand it!

It's so big, I don't know where to start!

As we've already seen, there are plenty of modern Bible translations that are easier to read than the more traditional ones.

But of course, there are still going to be tricky bits in the Bible, where the words might not make sense to you straight away. There are some parts where even the experts still debate the meaning of the text. But don't let that put you off. If you come across something you don't understand, make a note to yourself to look into it in more detail when you have time. The 'Connectives' in the next part of this book will help you, or you could simply ask someone who does understand to explain it to you. **And don't forget, there are many places in the Bible where the meaning is plain and simple and you can put it into action straight away.**

The Bible does contain a lot of writing; after all, it is (at least) 66 books in one, with around 773,000 words (GNB). But it has been broken down into bite-sized chunks – Old Testament and New Testament, with books, chapters and verses – that make it more manageable to read as much or as little as you would like. And wouldn't you expect the story of God and his people to feature more than just a few glossy magazine-style pages and some cartoons? Let's put it into perspective: JK Rowling's *Harry Potter and the Order of the Phoenix* has approximately 255,000 words in it, whereas the New Testament of the Good News Bible only has around 207,000.

If you're really stuck, start with the Gospel of Mark, the second book in the New Testament. This is short, snappy and all about Jesus.

The sample Bible studies later in *Inside Out* will get you off to a good start.

I find it boring!

In such a big book there are inevitably going to be some bits that are less interesting than others, but isn't that the same in any book we read? The Bible does contain some sections that seem a bit dull, such as lengthy family trees, measurements of buildings, lists of numbers and detailed laws.

But what about the emotional love stories, the brave action heroes, the inspirational friendships, the supernatural happenings, the fascinating history, the moving poems and the life-changing wisdom? **Don't get bogged down in a passage that you consider dull when there are many more exciting parts just over the page!**

How do I know it's true?

This is an excellent question and one which many people ask of the Bible. If this *is* a question that concerns you, it's best to do some research for yourself. You could start by watching the video 'Why trust the Bible?' at gnbyouthedition.co.uk/apologetics2. There is loads of evidence to find. For example, there are very early copies of the original text dating back to AD125.

Then there is the archaeological evidence for the places and events in the Bible; the consistency throughout the Bible, even though it was written by many different authors over about 1,400 years; and the incredible accuracy of many of the prophecies written in the Bible, especially those that were fulfilled by the coming of Jesus. Another important piece of evidence is the personal testimony of the effect of the Bible on people's lives.

It seems irrelevant to my life!

Many people do wonder how such an ancient book can be relevant to us today. After all, it was written thousands of years ago, to people with a vastly different culture, even speaking different languages.

But these people are startlingly similar to us in the things that really matter, such as life and death, love, peace, happiness, freedom and relationships. Many people believe that the Bible gives us the answers to the big questions that humans have been asking throughout the ages, such as why we are here, what we are supposed to do, and where we will end up in the future. We will see later in *Inside Out* how to make sense of the context in which the Bible was written, so as to draw out the principles that are still vitally relevant to us today.

The Bible says things I don't like!

There is no denying that the Bible is challenging and it can say some things that make us feel uncomfortable. The Bible is God's living word and sometimes God needs to challenge us, correct us or direct us as we continue on our journey of becoming more like Jesus – and that's a good thing!

There are also bits that it's OK not to like. For example, some of the writers of the Bible think there's no problem in keeping slaves. Also, there are Old Testament laws about how to treat women that we would consider quite wrong today. Again, this is where context is really important. Exploring where those ideas fit into the culture of the time and the overall story of the Bible will help us understand how to apply its truths to our lives today.

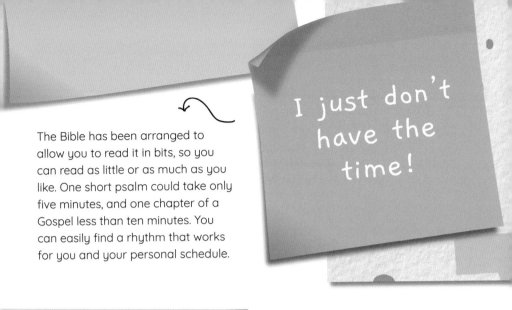

I just don't have the time!

The Bible has been arranged to allow you to read it in bits, so you can read as little or as much as you like. One short psalm could take only five minutes, and one chapter of a Gospel less than ten minutes. You can easily find a rhythm that works for you and your personal schedule.

Other people will think I'm weird if I read the Bible!

Well, some people might, but anyone who is a true friend will respect your beliefs and encourage you in them, especially if they start seeing some positive changes in your life. You must decide if it is more important to you to grow in your relationship with Jesus or be concerned about what others may or may not think of you.

BLESSINGS AND BENEFITS

The Bible talks about itself a lot! There are numerous verses that declare the importance and benefit of reading God's word for those who desire to grow as disciples of Jesus. The Bible often uses the terms like 'God's word', 'the Law' and 'Scriptures' to describe itself. Read the following verses (taken from the Good News Bible) and let the Bible speak!

2 TIMOTHY 3.16–17

All Scripture is inspired by God and is useful for teaching the truth, rebuking error, correcting faults, and giving instruction for right living, so that the person who serves God may be fully qualified and equipped to do every kind of good deed.

JOHN 8.31–32

So Jesus said to those who believed in him, 'If you obey my teaching, you are really my disciples; you will know the truth, and the truth will set you free.'

JOSHUA 1.8

'Be sure that the book of the Law is always read in your worship. Study it day and night, and make sure that you obey everything written in it. Then you will be prosperous and successful.'

HEBREWS 4.12

The word of God is alive and active, sharper than any double-edged sword. It cuts all the way through, to where soul and spirit meet, to where joints and marrow come together. It judges the desires and thoughts of the heart.

ACTS 20.32

'And now I commend you to the care of God and to the message of his grace, which is able to build you up and give you the blessings God has for all his people.'

MATTHEW 4.4

But Jesus answered, 'The scripture says, "Human beings cannot live on bread alone, but need every word that God speaks."'

ROMANS 15.4

Everything written in the Scriptures was written to teach us, in order that we might have hope through the patience and encouragement which the Scriptures give us.

PSALM 119.105

Your word is a lamp to guide me and a light for my path.

PSALM 119.11

I keep your law in my heart, so that I will not sin against you.

TRY READING THROUGH ALL THESE VERSES AGAIN. THIS TIME USE A PEN TO HIGHLIGHT ALL THE BLESSINGS AND BENEFITS THAT PEOPLE WHO REGULARLY READ GOD'S WORD RECEIVE.

THE BIBLE ALSO USES MANY DIFFERENT IMAGES TO DESCRIBE GOD'S WORD.

 Fire
Jeremiah 23.29

 Hammer
Jeremiah 23.29

 Lamp
Psalm 119.105

 Light
2 Peter 1.19

 Mirror
James 1.22–25

 Rod and staff
Psalm 23.4

 Sword
Ephesians 6.17; Hebrews 4.12

 Seed
Luke 8.11

 Food
Matthew 4.4

 Adviser
Psalm 119.24

Try reading the same passage from the Bible again and again over a few days. Each time you read it, approach it with a different word picture in your mind. What different things do you notice about the passage, depending on whether you are reading it as a 'mirror', 'hammer', 'sword' and so on?

THE INSIDE OUT CONNECTIVES

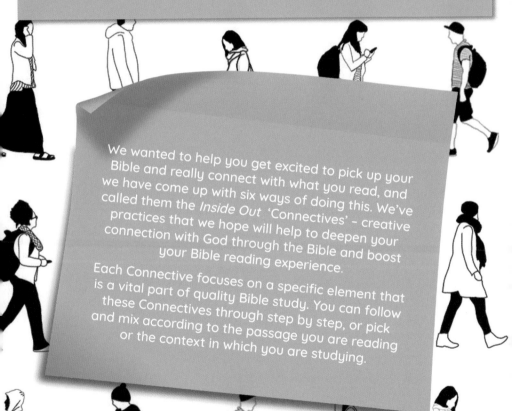

We wanted to help you get excited to pick up your Bible and really connect with what you read, and we have come up with six ways of doing this. We've called them the *Inside Out* 'Connectives' – creative practices that we hope will help to deepen your connection with God through the Bible and boost your Bible reading experience.

Each Connective focuses on a specific element that is a vital part of quality Bible study. You can follow these Connectives through step by step, or pick and mix according to the passage you are reading or the context in which you are studying.

THE SIX CONNECTIVES ARE:

Pray

Quite simply, remembering to pray when you read – before, during and after.

Read

There's no way around it: you've got to open the book and read the words. So the 'Read' Connective offers loads of suggestions to help you with the practicalities of reading and understanding the Bible text, from looking up Bible references to using daily Bible reading apps and commentaries.

Explore

The 'Explore' Connective takes you into the Bible text in more detail, to think about the context, timeline, language and principles underpinning the writing. This helps the words come alive before your very eyes.

Question

This Connective is all about investigating
Scripture through asking questions. Read
between the lines to uncover: What's going on?
What does it mean? Who's who? What can I
learn from them?

Dig

The 'Dig' Connective is about getting a part of the Bible
inside you. It could be a single word, a whole verse, the
meaning of a story or even the attitude of a character.
This Connective presents several different tools, such as
paraphrasing, meditating, memorising and storytelling, to
bring the Bible text to life in your life.

Live

The final Connective asks you to 'live' out the
words of the Bible in your life. This means finding
ways to action what you learn from Scripture on
a daily basis. Putting into action the words of the
Bible means thinking about how the words you
have read, explored, questioned and reflected on
make a practical difference in your normal life.
Are there any changes that you need to make?
Are there any actions that you need to take?

NOW that YOU'Ve Been introduced to the six connectives, JOt DOWN YOUR thoughts ABOUt them hERE. Then READ On...

THE INSIDE OUT CONNECTIVES

PRAY

Pray before, during and after your reading.

Reading the Bible is more than just reading text. The words in the Bible are God's living words and are one way that God uses to speak clearly and powerfully into our lives.

As you read the Bible, take time to pray and talk to God about his words on those pages. As you hear him speaking to you, it's natural to speak back, having a conversation with God. That's what God longs for you to do as you read his words. You can pray before, during and after your reading.

BEFORE YOU OPEN THE BOOK, ASK GOD TO BE WITH YOU AS YOU READ HIS WORD:

Ask him to guide you to the right passage

Pray that he will make the words come alive to you

Ask him to help you to understand what you are reading

During your reading, you can pray short prayers, like:

'WOW!'

'That's amazing'

'I DON'T GET IT'

'This is really challenging me'

'I NEVER KNEW THAT'

After you have finished reading:

- **ask** God how his words apply to you right now
- **ask** for help if you haven't understood
- **commit** to the challenge or change
- **accept** God's words of love, comfort and encouragement
- **thank** God for his wisdom

READ

Find your way round the Bible, search words and themes online and use Bible reading tools.

1200

Mark

....

Zephan.
Haggai
Zechar.
Malachi
Matt.

FINDING YOUR WAY AROUND

Every Bible will have a contents page at the start, with page numbers so that you can easily find the book you're looking for. Often there will also be an introduction page at the start of each book, giving a broad overview of the themes in the book and some handy background information, such as when and why it might have been written, and who might have written it.

The Bible text is broken into smaller chunks so that we can easily search for a particular part. Each book is split into chapters, and then each chapter is split into verses. So, if you see the reference Mark 16.1–5, this means the book of Mark, chapter 16, and verse 1 through to verse 5. The chapter numbers will be printed in large type, and the verse numbers will be printed much smaller.

31 In the same way the chief priests and the teachers of the Law jeered at Jesus, saying to each other, "He saved others, but he cannot save himself! 32 Let us see the Messiah, the king of Israel, come down from the cross now, and we will believe in him!"

And the two who were crucified with Jesus insulted him also.

The Death of Jesus
(Mt 27.45–56; Lk 23.44–49; Jn 19.28–30)

33 At noon the whole country was covered with darkness, which lasted for three hours. 34 At three o'clock Jesus cried out with a loud shout, "Eloi, Eloi, lema sabachthani?" which means, "My God, my God, why did you abandon me?"

35 Some of the people there heard him and said, "Listen, he is calling for Elijah!" 36 One of them ran up with a sponge, soaked it in cheap wine, and put it on the end of a stick. Then he held it up to Jesus' lips and said, "Wait! Let us see if Elijah is coming to bring him down from the cross!"

37 With a loud cry Jesus died.

38 The curtain hanging in the Temple was torn in two, from top to bottom. 39 The army officer who was standing there in front of the cross saw how Jesus had died.* "This man was really the Son of God!" he said.

40 Some women were there, looking on from a distance. Among them were Mary Magdalene, Mary the mother of the younger James and of Joseph, and Salome. 41 They had followed Jesus while he was in Galilee and had helped him. Many other women who had come to Jerusalem with him were there also.

The Burial of Jesus
(Mt 27.57–61; Lk 23.50–56; Jn 19.38–42)

42-43 It was towards evening when Joseph of Arimathea arrived. He was a respected member of the Council, who was waiting for the coming of the Kingdom of God. It was Preparation day (that is, the day before the Sabbath), so Joseph went boldly into the presence of Pilate and asked him for the body of Jesus. 44 Pilate was surprised to hear that Jesus was already dead. He called the army officer and asked him if Jesus had been dead a long time. 45 After hearing the officer's report, Pilate told Joseph he could have the body. 46 Joseph bought a linen sheet, took the body down, wrapped it in the sheet, and placed it in a tomb which had been dug out of solid rock. Then he rolled a large stone across the entrance to the tomb. 47 Mary Magdalene and Mary the mother of Joseph were watching and saw where the body of Jesus was placed.

The Resurrection
(Mt 28.1–8; Lk 24.1–12; Jn 20.1–10)

16 After the Sabbath was over, Mary Magdalene, Mary the mother of James, and Salome bought spices to go and anoint the body of Jesus. 2 Very early on Sunday morning, at sunrise, they went to the tomb. 3-4 On the way they said to one another, "Who will roll away the stone for us from the entrance to the tomb?" (It was a very large stone.) Then they looked up and saw that the stone had already been rolled back. 5 So they entered the tomb, where they saw a young man sitting on the right, wearing a white robe — and they were alarmed.

6 "Don't be alarmed," he said. "I know you are looking for Jesus of Nazareth, who was crucified. He is not here — he has been

....

15.39 had died; some manuscripts have had cried out and died.

HOW TO BEGIN

Most people find that it's not the best idea to start from the beginning of the Bible and try to read it all the way through, from cover to cover! *The Good News Bible – Youth Edition* (page 11) suggests some good places to start:

- the Gospel of Mark – the shortest and most action-packed version of the story of Jesus

- the book of Proverbs – full of wisdom for life, and you can read just one verse at a time

- the book of Psalms – poetic and easy to read, they span the whole range of human emotion

Or you could decide how much time you've got:

- **5 minutes** – pick just one story from a Gospel or a single psalm

- **15 minutes** – pray first, then read one chapter from a book. Read it again, underline bits, ask questions, colour and think about what it means for you

- **30 minutes** – read a longer chapter or a few chapters back to back. If you have this much time, use one of the other Connectives to help you read more carefully

Bible Book Club

The Bible Society's Bible Book Club provides a neat summary of all the books of the Bible, including handy background information, discussion questions and some hints for handling any tricky sections.

biblesociety.org.uk/bookclub

The Bible Project

The Bible Project produces short animated videos to make the biblical story accessible to everyone. Many of the videos give an overview of the different books of the Bible and show how the Bible li nks together to form one unified story. There are also some cool posters that are free to download.

thebibleproject.com

Bible searching

You can use a Bible search engine if you want to know what the Bible says about a particular topic (for example, forgiveness), or if you can remember a few words of a Bible passage but can't remember where to find it.

One great website to use is **biblegateway.com**. This site lets you search for a word or theme, or for a particular Bible reference, in many different English translations (and in some other languages as well). It also offers study guides, daily reading plans and even an audio Bible app.

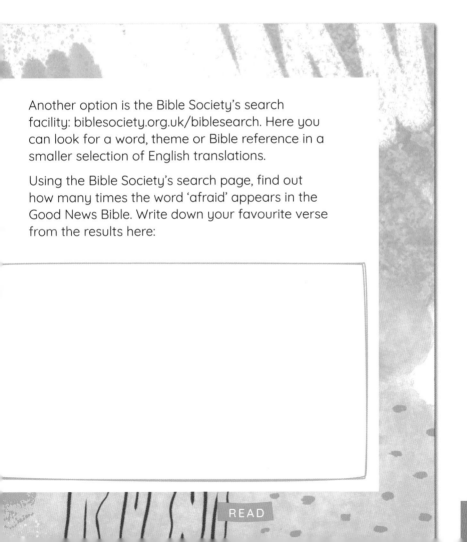

Another option is the Bible Society's search facility: biblesociety.org.uk/biblesearch. Here you can look for a word, theme or Bible reference in a smaller selection of English translations.

Using the Bible Society's search page, find out how many times the word 'afraid' appears in the Good News Bible. Write down your favourite verse from the results here:

READ

Now search for two more words of your choice.

Word:	Word:
How many times?	How many times?
My favourite verse from the results:	My favourite verse from the results:

DAILY BIBLE READING TOOLS

Daily Bible reading notes provide you with a daily Scripture reading, plus an explanation, questions, thoughts and/or stories and often a prayer to help you apply the passage to your day. There are loads out there to choose from and so many different formats, from booklets to apps and podcasts, with many written specifically for young people. These are well worth investing in as it is an easy step into the habit of daily Bible reading. *The Good News Bible – Youth Edition* has three Bible reading plans on pages 19 and 20, with supporting videos online, to get you started.

SOME APPS THAT WE LIKE ARE:

The Word for You Today

This app provides a short daily Scripture reading with thoughts for reflection and ideas for action.

YouVersion Bible Lens

The YouVersion Bible Lens app suggests Bible verses to match with your own photos and produces images that can then be shared on social media.

Daily Lyfe

This Bible Society app provides a short Scripture to read and reflect on every day – morning, lunchtime and in the evening.

A Bible commentary is an extra book that you can use if you want to understand a particular passage of the Bible in more depth. Perhaps you want to know more about the history, the context, or what different theologians think it means. You can get Bible commentaries that cover the whole of the Bible, or those that look at just one book. Tom Wright writes some excellent commentaries in his 'For Everyone' series.

READ

EXPLORE

Think about the language, timeline, context and principles underpinning the biblical text, to help it come alive.

EXPLORE THE LANGUAGE

The Bible was not written in English. When people translated it from Hebrew, Greek or Aramaic into English, they had to find the English word that best corresponded to the original meaning. Sometimes there simply isn't an English word that does this, so looking at different Bible translations (perhaps using biblegateway.com), or even researching back to the original language, can help make sense of the Bible.

EXPLORE THE TIMELINE

We also need to understand how any individual Bible passage or story fits into the whole biblical story and how it is part of the overall plan. The first 17 books of the Old Testament (the historical books) tell the story of the Israelites in roughly the order that the events happened (called 'chronological order'), but the remaining 22 books of poetry and prophecy are not part of this order. The letters in the New Testament are not in chronological order, either.

For that reason, it can be helpful to have a timeline of the Bible. You can see a timeline in the *Good News Bible – Youth Edition*: look at pages 14 to 17 for highlights from this one big story. You can also download this timeline from biblesociety.org.uk/youthbible (scroll down to 'Extras').

EXPLORE THE CONTEXT

To understand the full meaning behind the Bible text, we sometimes need to look into the context – what the world was like at the time the authors were writing, and what those words would have meant to the people who first heard them.

Let's look at an example.

Start by reading John 4.1–26, the story of Jesus meeting the Samaritan woman at a well in Samaria. Jot down your thoughts about what you feel this text is saying:

On the surface, this story appears quite straightforward, but for the people who first heard about this encounter, it was shocking and revolutionary. Let's discover why.

In verse 4 the text says that Jesus 'had to' go through Samaria

In fact, when travelling from Judea to Galilee, as Jesus and his disciples were, it was *not* necessary to go through Samaria. The Jews and the Samaritans did not get along. They had different religious beliefs, and the Jews viewed the Samaritans as an 'unclean' marginalised people group. Jewish travellers normally travelled around Samaria, making a detour of several days, just to avoid coming into contact with them. But Jesus *chose* to journey directly through that very region.

Verses 6 and 7 tell us that around midday Jesus rested by a well, and a woman came to the well to draw water.

This is unusual because the women would usually go to collect their water together, either early in the morning or later in the evening, when the sun was coolest. Why was this woman on her own at the hottest part of the day? She appears as a lonely figure, an outcast from her community, with no one else in the family to draw the water for her.

Jesus broke all sorts of cultural rules to speak to this woman. At that time in history, women were seen as inferior to men. They had no rights, and a Jewish man did not talk with women in the street, not even with his wife. Also, Jewish people did not associate with Samaritan people, who were viewed as outcasts and unclean.

Now we understand why what Jesus did here was so shocking to the people around him, even to the woman herself. He did something that was a cultural taboo: he spoke to a woman in public – and not just any woman, but a Samaritan woman. Jesus asked her for a drink of water. She was doubly shocked by that: a Jewish man was speaking to her, and now he even wanted to share her cup of water?

The conversation continued and eventually (verse 26) Jesus told the women who he was.

This Samaritan woman was the first person to whom Jesus openly revealed himself as Messiah. She then went and told her people about Jesus and brought them to him, so that they could see and hear for themselves – making her the first evangelist in the Gospel of John.

Look back at the notes you made on page 33. Now that you understand more of the context behind this story, how have your thoughts changed?

EXPLORE THE TRUTHS FOR TODAY

Although the world has changed since the Bible was written, God hasn't! Sometimes we have to delve beneath the face value of the text to draw out the principles of God and his word. There may be times when the Bible doesn't *appear* to relate to us in our culture today, but if we dig deep enough, we will uncover spiritual truths that can still guide, inform and bless us today.

Think again about the story of Jesus meeting the Samaritan woman. At first glance this story seems a world away from our modern-day society, yet there are still some incredible truths we can take on board.

For example:

- Jesus sees us as we are, loves us and wants to be with us, regardless of how we feel about ourselves.

- Jesus is the only person who can truly satisfy the deep 'thirst' we have in our lives – to belong, to be accepted, to be loved, to be known.

- Jesus reaches out to all people, regardless of race or class or anything else that may make them different or marginalised.

- Jesus crosses barriers, rules and traditions to share the gospel.

What other truths can you take away from this story?

What one truth can you put into action in your life right now?

QUESTION ?

Investigate Scripture through asking questions. Read between the lines to uncover the answers: What's going on? What does it mean? Who's who? What can I learn from them?

THERE ARE THREE TYPES OF QUESTION WE CAN ASK TO HELP US UNDERSTAND THE BIBLE TEXT:

Understanding: What do the words and phrases actually mean and how do I understand what they say?

Observation: Searching for facts such as who, what, when, why and where? These questions are useful when looking into the context of the passage.

Action: What actions should I take? What commands are there to obey? What promises are there to remember?

SIX QUESTIONS

One well-known method of studying a Bible text is by using the following six symbols. Simply write or draw the symbols down the side of a piece of paper and ask yourself the corresponding questions about the Bible passage you are reading. Jot down your thoughts as you go along.

 What do these verses tell you about God/Jesus?

 What do these verses tell you about human nature, about people?

 What do you think is the most exciting verse in this passage, and why?

 Is there anything you don't understand or want to find out more about?

 Have you made any new discoveries through reading these verses?

 How do these verses affect your life today? What would you like to do or change in your life in response?

Give it a try with Mark 10.46–52, where blind Bartimaeus receives his sight, and Mark 5.21–43, where Jesus heals a 12-year-old girl and a woman. You can do this either on your own or in a group where you can discuss your answers.

Write down your thoughts on the next two pages.

Mark 5.21–43

Now jot down your thoughts about this method of Bible study.

- Did the questions help you consider the passage in a deeper way?

- Did you find it easy or difficult to answer the questions?

- Did you find yourself asking other questions about the text?

- Did this exercise enable you to discover new ways to live out the challenges, promises or commands that you have just read?

FOCUS on Jesus

The Gospels (Matthew, Mark, Luke and John) tell us about the life and teachings of Jesus. We can learn so much from the Bible text in these books by focusing on Jesus – thinking about how he lived his life, the things that he said, and how people were changed by meeting him.

Here are some questions to help you:

- Where is Jesus and who is he with?

- What does Jesus do, and why?

- What does Jesus say, and how does he say it?

- How do others respond to Jesus? What do they learn and how are their lives changed by meeting with him?

- What actions can you take in response to what you have read? What is Jesus saying or doing that could change your life? What could you share with others?

- What are the 'wow' moments?

Try answering these questions with any of the following Bible passages:

- Mark 6.30–44 (Jesus feeds a great crowd)

- Mark 11.1–11 (The triumphant entry into Jerusalem)

- Mark 11.15–19 (Jesus goes to the temple)

- Mark 14.3–9 (Jesus is anointed at Bethany)

Use the space on the following page for your answers.

NOTES

WHAT DOES THE BIBLE SAY ABOUT _____?

You can also approach the Bible by looking at different themes, asking, 'What does the Bible say about _____?' For example, you could study grace, forgiveness, worry, love or faith. A good tool for this kind of questioning is a Bible dictionary or the websites we've already mentioned – biblegateway.com or biblesociety.org.uk/biblesearch. These will allow you to do a keyword search. Read around the Scriptures that you find, think about the context, and draw out the common threads that you can put into action.

The *Good News Bible – Youth Edition* has pulled together key Bible verses on several 'Big Issues' in the back pages, such as bullying, the environment, and mental health.

CHARACTER STUDY

You can use a similar approach in doing a character study, asking the question, 'What can I learn from the story of _____?' Pick someone who interests or inspires you from a Bible story and then use an online resource to find out what is written about them in the Bible. Read the person's story, explore the context of his or her life, and ask questions such as:

- What strengths does this person show?
- What is their relationship with God like?
- How did they respond to trouble or hardship?
- What mistakes did they make and how did they learn from those mistakes?
- What encourages or inspires me about this person's life?
- What can I learn from their story?

TRY THIS WITH THE STORY OF RAHAB AND THE SPIES IN JOSHUA 2.

Read the whole of Joshua chapter 2 and Hebrews 11.31. Then do a little online research on 'Rahab and the spies'. For example, see if you can find a character profile for Rahab or some study notes on Joshua 2. It would also help to read Joshua 1, to set the context for Rahab's involvement in this story. Look as well at any pictures that may help to make the story more vivid for you.

Make some notes from your research here:

Now consider the following questions:

- What strengths did Rahab show?
- What was her relationship with God like?
- How did Rahab respond to trouble and fear?
- What encourages or inspires you about Rahab's life?
- What can you learn from her story?
- What does this story tell you about who God chooses to work through?
- What situations do you face where you would be frightened to 'do the right thing'?
- What one question would you like to ask Rahab if you met her at this time in her life?

Use the space on the following page for your answers.

NOTES

QUESTION

DIG

Get the Bible inside you by
paraphrasing, meditating,
memorising, storytelling
and more.

Paraphrasing

Paraphrasing can be a really useful way of getting behind the meaning
of the words. It means using your own words to express the essence
of the Scripture passage. Be careful not to change the meaning; just
communicate it in a different manner, using words and contexts that are
more familiar to you. The Message or The Living Bible are good examples
of a paraphrase.

2 Timothy 3.16–17 says, 'All Scripture is inspired by God and is useful
for teaching the truth, rebuking error, correcting faults, and giving
instruction for right living, so that the person who serves God may be
fully qualified and equipped to do every kind of good deed.'

This could be paraphrased as follows: 'The whole Bible is inspired by God
and is important to teach us the truth and help us to understand where
we are going wrong in our lives. It shows us how to live holy lives. It builds
us up and gets us ready to do whatever it is that God has planned for us.'

Be sure that the book of the Law is always read in your worship. Study it day and night, and make sure that you obey everything written in it. Then you will be prosperous and successful. (Joshua 1.8)

My paraphrase:

You created every part of me; you put me together in my mother's womb. I praise you because you are to be feared; all you do is strange and wonderful. I know it with all my heart. (Psalm 139.13–14)

My paraphrase:

There is no condemnation now for those who live in union with Christ Jesus. For the law of the Spirit, which brings us life in union with Christ Jesus, has set me free from the law of sin and death. (Romans 8.1–2)

My paraphrase:

Meditating

Christian meditation is a way of allowing Scripture to fill our mind, and of hearing God speak to us through it. It is not the same as Eastern mysticism, which is more about trying to empty our minds. Meditation demands discipline, as our minds tend to wander off the topic, but it is a fantastic way of uncovering the truths in Scripture in a way that can make a big impact on our lives.

1. Position yourself in a comfortable, quiet **place** where you won't be distracted (or fall asleep!)

2. Spend a minute or two focusing on your **breathing**, allowing your mind to concentrate.

3. **Pray**: ask God to be with you and speak to you through your meditation.

4. **Read** the Scripture slowly and thoughtfully, several times. (Reading aloud, or even writing out the words, may help you to stay focused.) Each time you read it, emphasise a different word.

5. Allow your thoughts to be drawn to a specific word, phrase or sentence and follow that train of thought. Listen for God's voice in your thoughts. You might **notice** something that you have never seen before, or experience an emotion such as peace, happiness or amazement.

6. **Pray** about what you are thinking or feeling. If your mind wanders off, don't worry, just start again.

The LORD our Shepherd*

23 ¹The LORD is my shepherd;
I have everything I need.
² He lets me rest in fields of green grass
and leads me to quiet pools of fresh water.
³ He gives me new strength.
He guides me in the right paths,
as he has promised.
⁴ Even if I go through the deepest darkness,
I will not be afraid, LORD,
for you are with me.
Your shepherd's rod and staff protect me.

⁵ You prepare a banquet for me,
where all my enemies can see me;
you welcome me as an honoured guest
and fill my cup to the brim.
⁶ I know that your goodness and love will be with me all my
life;
and your house will be my home as long as I live.

You could also try Psalm 139.13–18; Matthew 6.25–34; 1 Corinthians 13.1–13; Philippians 1.6.

Memorising

Memorising Scripture fills your mind and heart with the truths of the Bible and gets them right inside you. Then they are immediately accessible when you (or a friend) need comfort, encouragement, help or guidance – or just want to praise God. In countries today where owning a Bible is illegal, followers of Jesus memorise large sections of Scripture, so they always have God's words with them.

Even if you have a terrible memory, you can still train yourself to remember verses of the Bible. The best way to memorise is to break the passage into portions. Say each portion out loud so that you can hear it as well as see it and think it. When you have got the first part, learn the second bit, and then try to recite the first and second parts together, and so on until you have remembered the whole Scripture. Say it the same way each time.

Try writing out the passage several times to help you remember it. You could also record it and listen to the recording over and over, whispering along with the words. If you are musical or creative, sing the verse, rap it, draw it, or even act it out.

For inspiration, search 'Ryan Ferguson recites' on YouTube. This guy gives dramatic memorised recitation of Psalms and other parts of Scripture.

One way to keep a verse on your mind would be to set it as your home or lock screen, or pop a Post-it note inside your phone case, so that you read it every time you unlock your phone. Quote the verses often, asking God for deeper understanding and seeking to apply each verse to your life.

Now have a go at memorising 1 Thessalonians 5.16–18:

> **Be joyful always, pray at all times, be thankful in all circumstances. This is what God wants from you in your life in union with Christ Jesus.**

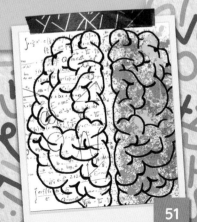

You could also try:
- Matthew 5.13–16
- Psalm 150
- 1 Peter 5.6–7
- Isaiah 41.8–10

USE YOUR IMAGINATION

As you are reading a Bible passage, imagine you are there in the scene, as a bystander or one of the main characters. What can you hear, see and smell? How do you feel? What are you thinking about? How would you respond to the situation going on around you?

In a group, each person could focus on a different character from the text and then describe to the other group members what it was like being that person.

Try this with the healing of blind Bartimaeus (Mark 10.46–52), which we looked at using the 'Question' Connective.

*Imagine you are in the crowd on your way out of Jericho with Jesus. You're all walking slowly because it's **hot and dusty** on the pathway. Everyone is very excited, though, because you're going up to Jerusalem for a big festival. Then, above all the chatter, you hear a man's voice **shouting** for Jesus' attention.*

*Can you see the man? Do you know him? Or do you just hear others saying it's Bartimaeus, the **blind beggar** who always sits at that place by the side of the road? How do you feel to hear him yelling at the top of his voice? Embarrassed? Annoyed? Frightened? Sorry for him?*

*Then everyone comes to a standstill while Jesus turns back to speak to the man. Can you hear their conversation? How do you feel when you realise that Bartimaeus is suddenly **no longer blind**? Jesus has healed him! What is the atmosphere like in the crowd as the once-blind beggar joins you on the way to Jerusalem?*

*Now go back to the beginning of the story and imagine yourself as the blind man. How long have you been blind? What do you do all day? Imagine hearing the noisy crowd approaching. What you do think when you find out that it's Jesus who is with them? How do you feel when other people tell you to stop calling out? What makes you **keep on shouting**? And what is it like when you actually come to Jesus and, amazingly, find that you can see? What will your **life be like** from this day on?*

STORYTELLING

Storytelling is another way to stimulate our imagination and help us connect to the Bible text and make it relevant in our lives today. Jesus used storytelling in his teaching all the time. We now call those stories 'parables'.

Try to rewrite a Bible story in your own words, either in its original setting or putting it into a 21st-century context. Use modern words and phrases but be sure not to change the meaning. You could take your story out to read in the environment where it is set – for example, the seashore, a hillside, a streamside path or a dirt track.

Have a go with the story of the good Samaritan (Luke 10.25–37), the unforgiving servant (Matthew 18.23–35) or Jesus walking on the water (Mark 6.45–56).

Image and art

If you like to paint or draw or model, use these skills to create images about the verses you have read. Create something that ties the action in the text together with the meaning behind it. Or compose a piece that reflects your feelings on reading the words, or the emotions of someone involved in the story. Share your work of art with others, as it will definitely speak to them about God in exciting new ways.

Try this with John 14.1–6:

'Do not be worried and upset,' Jesus told them. 'Believe in God and believe also in me. There are many rooms in my Father's house, and I am going to prepare a place for you. I would not tell you this if it were not so. And after I go and prepare a place for you, I will come back and take you to myself, so that you will be where I am. You know the way that leads to the place where I am going.' Thomas said to him, 'Lord, we do not know where you are going; so how can we know the way to get there?' Jesus answered him, 'I am the way, the truth, and the life; no one goes to the Father except by me.'

If you are stuck for ideas, try drawing a picture of your house and then decorating it with the promises from this passage.

Other Scriptures you could try to draw are:

- Jeremiah 17.7–8
- John 15.5–10
- Galatians 5.1

If you really can't draw, try an internet image search about the passage. Read about Jesus washing his disciples' feet in John 13.2–17. Then take a look at this painting by Nicolas Bertin. Does it illustrate anything to you about the story? Does it draw out different thoughts and feelings from you than simply reading the Bible text? How and why?

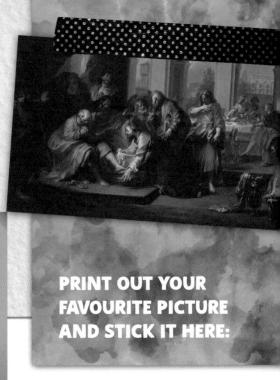

Try this with the following Bible passages.

- Luke 15.4–7 (the parable of the lost sheep)

- Mark 2.1–12 (Jesus heals a paralysed man)

- Galatians 5.1

PRINT OUT YOUR FAVOURITE PICTURE AND STICK IT HERE:

If you like photos, try creating a photo storyboard by taking or creating several images that represent 'stills' of the Bible text. Use these images to meditate and pray through the text and allow God to speak to you about its meaning for you today.

One final idea: look on YouTube for someone else's visual interpretation of what you are reading. You will probably find a very diverse offering, including text simply set to music, animations, short homemade films, children reading the Scriptures, and the Bible in other languages. You could even create your own.

STORYBOARD:

SCRIBBLESTORM

If you prefer words, print out a large sheet of the text (you could get this from biblegateway.com if you don't want to type it out yourself) and read it again and again. As you notice repeated words or themes, link phrases together with coloured pens or highlighters, make notes to help you understand the purpose, and jot down comments along the side about how it makes you feel. This is how it could be done:

Must have been squashed!

Whose house was this, and how big?

A few days later Jesus went back to Capernaum, and the news spread that he was at home. ²So many people came together that there was no room left, not even out in front of the door. Jesus was preaching the message to them ³when four men arrived, carrying a paralysed man to Jesus. ⁴Because of the crowd, however, they could not get the man to him. So they made a hole in the roof right above the place where Jesus was. When they had made an opening, they let the man down, lying on his mat. ⁵Seeing how much faith they had, Jesus said to the paralysed man, 'My son, your sins are forgiven.'

How long did this take?

The friends showed their faith in a practical way.

⁶Some teachers of the Law who were sitting there thought to themselves, ⁷'How does he dare talk like this? This is blasphemy! God is the only one who can forgive sins!'

These guys were here to test Jesus or catch him out.

Jesus' words bring miraculous healing. He didn't even have to touch the man.

Wow!

⁸At once Jesus knew what they were thinking, so he said to them, 'Why do you think such things? ⁹Is it easier to say to this paralysed man, "Your sins are forgiven," or to say, "Get up, pick up your mat, and walk"? ¹⁰I will prove to you, then, that the Son of Man has authority on earth to forgive sins.' So he said to the paralysed man, ¹¹'I tell you, get up, pick up your mat, and go home!'

¹²While they all watched, the man got up, picked up his mat, and hurried away. They were all completely amazed and praised God, saying, 'We have never seen anything like this!'

MARK 2.1-12

Nor me!

So did they also end up praising God?

You could even do this in your Bible. The *Good News Bible – Youth Edition* has large spaces at the side of each page for you to jot down your thoughts or prayers, doodle and colour, as well as some short journalling activities to help you get the most out of the words on the pages.

You could also download the scrapbook words and posters from biblesociety.org.uk/youthbible (scroll down to 'Extra stuff'), cut them out and stick them on to your Bible text to enhance your scribblestorm.

Try this with Philippians 2.5–11:

The attitude you should have is the
one that Christ Jesus had:
He always had the nature of God,
but he did not think that by force he
should try to remain equal with God.
Instead of this, of his own free will
he gave up all he had,
and took the nature of a servant.
He became like a human being
and appeared in human likeness.
He was humble and walked the path
of obedience all the way to death
his death on the cross.
For this reason God raised him to the
highest place above
and gave him the name that is
greater than any other name.
And so, in honour of the name
of Jesus
all beings in heaven, on earth, and in
the world below
will fall on their knees,
and all will openly proclaim that Jesus
Christ is Lord,
to the glory of God the Father.

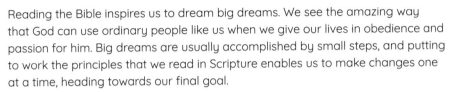

LIVE

Find ways of putting into action the words of the Bible, to make a practical difference in your everyday life.

Reading the Bible inspires us to dream big dreams. We see the amazing way that God can use ordinary people like us when we give our lives in obedience and passion for him. Big dreams are usually accomplished by small steps, and putting to work the principles that we read in Scripture enables us to make changes one at a time, heading towards our final goal.

The key thing in living the Bible is to be real in the way you apply it. It's great to think of massive ideas such as 'I need to love everyone I meet' but how will you know if you have achieved it? Try this instead: 'I will show my little brother something of Jesus' love this week by being kind to him and helping him with his homework.' You need to have a clear idea of what action you are going to take from the minute you put down your Bible. And don't forget to note down exactly what actions you are going to make and keep yourself accountable.

TRY THINKING ABOUT THE FOLLOWING QUESTIONS:

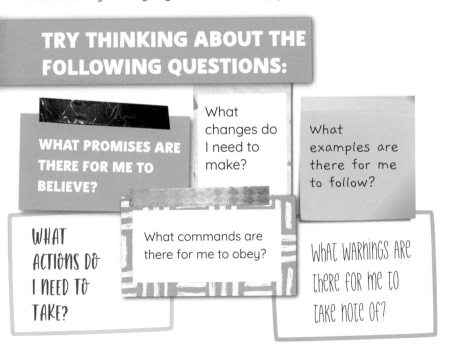

WHAT PROMISES ARE THERE FOR ME TO BELIEVE?

What changes do I need to make?

What examples are there for me to follow?

WHAT ACTIONS DO I NEED TO TAKE?

What commands are there for me to obey?

WHAT WARNINGS ARE THERE FOR ME TO TAKE NOTE OF?

don't have to write something for each question every time. As we said before, both small changes and big dreams are worth going after.

my own life?

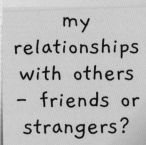

my relationship with God?

HOW WILL I ACTION THE TRUTHS OF THE BIBLE IN...

my relationships with others – friends or strangers?

my interaction in God's world?

Let's think again about the story of the healing of blind Bartimaeus (Mark 10.46–52). How could we action the truths we discovered in this story in our own lives?

MY OWN LIFE?

When I feel a bit like blind Bartimaeus, alone or rejected or without hope, I will remind myself that Jesus loves me, has time for me, and will provide everything I need. I will memorise verses 49 and 50, where Jesus asks Bartimaeus to come and be with him.

MY RELATIONSHIP WITH GOD?

There is one thing that God has promised me that I haven't yet seen fulfilled. I will start to pray about this again and trust God that he will do all that he has promised.

HOW WILL I ACTION THE TRUTHS OF THE BIBLE IN...

MY RELATIONSHIPS WITH OTHERS?

God values each individual. Tomorrow I will say hello to the person at school that no one usually talks to.

MY INTERACTION IN GOD'S WORLD?

I will take time to appreciate the beauty of God's creation. I will also research a charity that works to restore sight to the blind, and see if I can do anything to help.

NOTES

LIVE

GROUP BIBLE STUDIES

One of the great ways to discover the riches inside the Bible is to do it with friends. Meeting with other people to study the Bible can help you discover God in new ways and help you grow as a disciple of Jesus. A small group of people can read the same passage from the Bible and all have different thoughts or opinions, and in this way can learn from each other. Other people may notice something about the passage that you wouldn't have thought about, or they may have questions that you can help answer. A group of friends can also encourage and motivate each other to put God's word into practice and keep each other accountable in the actions they have committed to.

This part of *Inside Out* contains four short Bible studies, showing you how to use just some of the ideas described in the six 'Connectives' on pages 21–61. You can do these studies on your own, but we recommend that you do them with others. They shouldn't need too much preparation; just grab your friends, find a place without distraction, and bring your Bible, some pens and access to the internet.

GROUP BIBLE STUDY 1

Mark 2.1–12:
Jesus heals a
paralysed man

Pray

Ask God to be with you and help you to understand what you are reading. Tell him that you would like to uncover something new in the words.

Read

Read Mark 2.1–12 from a Bible. (If you are with friends, one person can read this out loud.)

Explore

Do an online picture search for 'houses in Bible times' to understand how the four men could easily have made a hole in the roof and lowered their friend through.

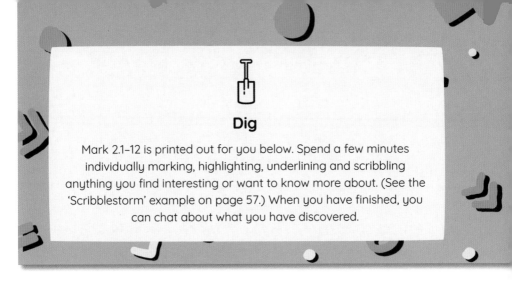

Dig

Mark 2.1–12 is printed out for you below. Spend a few minutes individually marking, highlighting, underlining and scribbling anything you find interesting or want to know more about. (See the 'Scribblestorm' example on page 57.) When you have finished, you can chat about what you have discovered.

A few days later Jesus went back to Capernaum, and the news spread that he was at home. So many people came together that there was no room left, not even out in front of the door. Jesus was preaching the message to them when four men arrived, carrying a paralysed man to Jesus. Because of the crowd, however, they could not get the man to him. So they made a hole in the roof right above the place where Jesus was. When they had made an opening, they let the man down, lying on his mat. Seeing how much faith they had, Jesus said to the paralysed man, 'My son, your sins are forgiven.'

Some teachers of the Law who were sitting there thought to themselves, 'How does he dare to talk like this? This is blasphemy! God is the only one who can forgive sins!'

At once Jesus knew what they were thinking, so he said to them, 'Why do you think such things? Is it easier to say to this paralysed man, "Your sins are forgiven", or to say, "Get up, pick up your mat, and walk"? I will prove to you, then, that the Son of Man has authority on earth to forgive sins.' So he said to the paralysed man, 'I tell you, get up, pick up your mat, and go home!'

While they all watched, the man got up, picked up his mat, and hurried away. They were all completely amazed and praised God, saying, 'We have never seen anything like this!'

Question

Are there any questions you would like to ask about this story? Share them with your friends and listen to their answers. Here are some other questions you could chat about ...

- Whose house was this? How would you respond if it were your house?
- Why did Jesus first say to the man, 'Your sins are forgiven'?
- How did the religious leaders react to this statement?
- What does this story teach us about being persistent in our prayers?
- What's the craziest thing you have ever done for a friend and why?
- Do you have good friends who support you in times of difficulty and need?
- How do you act when you see someone – friend or stranger – in need?

Pray

Thank God for his words in the Bible. Thank him for the example of faith that these four friends have given us. Pray for any members of your group who may be going through a hard time at the moment and imagine that you are bringing them before Jesus, just as these friends did for the paralysed man. Ask Jesus to increase your faith and help you put your faith into action.

Live

Discuss together and write down three things you have discovered from this passage that can make a difference to you. Decide on one practical action or change you can make in your own life in response to what you have read.

NOTES

Write your answers to
the questions here.

Group Bible Study 2

Pray

Ask God to be with you and help you to understand what you are reading. Tell him that you would like to uncover something new in the words.

Read

Read Matthew 14.22–32 from a Bible. (If you are with friends, one person can read this out loud.)

Question

You could use the six symbols on page 38 to ask six questions about this Bible passage. If you are with friends, you can discuss each question together, but make sure everyone gets a chance to contribute.

 What do these verses tell us about Jesus?

 What do these verses tell us about human nature, about people?

What do you think is the most exciting verse in this passage, and why?

Is there anything you don't understand or want to find out more about?

Have you made any new discoveries through reading these verses?

How do these verses affect your life today? What would you like to do or change in your life in response?

If you prefer, you could do a character study of Peter (see page 44), using the following questions:

- What strengths did Peter show?
- What was his relationship with Jesus like?
- How did Peter respond to trouble and fear?
- What mistakes did he make and how did he learn from those mistakes?
- How do you think Peter would have replied when Jesus asked him, 'Why did you doubt'?
- What encourages or inspires you about Peter's actions in this passage?

 ### Dig

Search on YouTube for a sound effects video of a storm, or watch a video of a stormy sea.

As you watch, imagine what it would be like to be in a small boat out on the sea, 'tossed about by the waves'.

 ### Live

Is there anything going on in your life at the moment that is a bit like a frightening storm on the sea? What can you do to show that you trust Jesus to bring you through it? Write or draw something here as a reminder of what you could change in your life. Write out Jesus' words in verse 27.

Pray

Thank God for his words in the Bible. Thank him that we can learn so much from the life of Peter. Ask Jesus to help you become more like Peter – to be able to take a step of faith into great adventures with him. Pray for any of your group who may feel like they are in a 'storm' at the moment. Ask Jesus to be with them in the boat and to calm the storm.

NOTES

GROUP BIBLE STUDY 3

 Pray

Ask God to be with you and help you to understand what you are reading. Tell him that you would like to uncover something new in the words.

 Read

Read John 6.1–15 from a Bible. (If you are with friends, one person can read this out loud.)

 Explore

Explore the context of this story with an online search:

- Find a map of Palestine in Bible times and look for Lake Galilee (in the north of the country). Can you decide which side of the lake Jesus was on when he fed this great crowd? (Look at John 6.16–17 for a clue.)

- Search for 'barley loaves in the Bible' and see what you can find out about this food. Was it eaten by the rich or the poor?

Question

Look closely at Jesus in the story. Use these questions about Jesus to study the things he said and did. Then look at the other people and think about how they responded to Jesus on this occasion.

- Where is Jesus and who is he with?
- What does Jesus do, and why?
- What does Jesus say, and how does he say it?
- How do others respond to Jesus? What do they learn and how are their lives changed by meeting with him?
- What is Jesus saying or doing that could change your life? What could you share with others?
- What are the 'wow' moments?

Live

Now draw out some practical actions for your own life, asking yourself, 'What examples are there for me to follow in this passage?'

- You could think about the two disciples, Philip and Andrew, who speak to Jesus in the story. Which of them sets a better example, and what could you learn from them?

- Is there anything small that you could offer to Jesus, like the young boy did with his loaves and fishes, which he could use to make a big difference?

Write some notes here, or draw a picture.

Pray

Thank God for his words in the Bible. Thank him that each one of us has an important part in his plan and story for the world. Commit yourself to playing your part, no matter what the cost.

GROUP BIBLE STUDY 4

Mark 10.17-25: The rich young man

Pray

Ask God to be with you and help you to understand what you are reading. Tell him that you would like to uncover something new in the words.

Read

Read Mark 10.17-25 from a Bible. (If you are with friends, one person can read this out loud.)

Explore

To understand why this passage is so important in the story of Jesus, we need to know that the rich man would have been well-respected and admired in his community because of his wealth. In Jewish culture, a person's wealth could be a sign of God's favour. This young man claims that he has never broken God's law, so it seems right that he should be rewarded with riches. But Jesus challenges this belief by telling him to sell everything he owns, give the money away, and put following Jesus first in his life.

Dig

Use your imagination to get inside the story of
the rich young man. One person in the group can
read this retelling, while the others listen carefully
and imagine themselves at the scene.

You are among the group of disciples, just about to leave town with Jesus. But then you see a young man running up to Jesus and kneeling at his feet. You look more closely and see that this man, although young, is very wealthy. He is wearing fine clothes, and there are the kind of whispers in the crowd around that tell you he is a well-respected person in the local community. He's rich, so he must be a very good man, highly favoured by God. So why is he on his knees at the feet of Jesus? What can he possibly want to say? You lean in closer to listen. 'Good Teacher,' he asks, 'what must I do to receive eternal life?' Now imagine that you are the rich young man. You realise that Jesus is about to leave town so you have grabbed your last chance to speak to him before he's gone. You have an important question to ask. Although you know that God has blessed you with riches in this life, you are still unsure about what happens after you die.

Jesus replies at first with a list of the commandments you should have kept. That's OK: you've never broken these or any of the other Jewish laws (all 613 of them!), so it seems you've done enough. You can relax!

But now Jesus is saying something else: 'Go and sell all you have and give the money to the poor, and you will have riches in heaven; then come and follow me.'

What an invitation! To submit your whole life to Jesus, follow him and have riches in heaven for ever!

But you can't do it. Your face stricken with grief, you rise from your knees. You take your eyes off Jesus, turn slowly, and move away from the group of disciples. You've turned down the invitation. You thought you wanted to follow Jesus but when it's come to the crunch you've walked away.

Why do you think the rich young man did this?

He had something in his life that he loved more than Jesus and he was not prepared to leave it behind and submit his whole life to follow him. Jesus' challenge went right to the heart of the man. He had to decide whether he was willing to give up the things that meant most to him – wealth and status within the community – as well as his belief that these things were a sign of God's blessing. But his riches were too important to him; they got in the way and he missed the opportunity of a lifetime.

Create a picture using colours to interpret how the rich young man might have felt after speaking with Jesus.

TRY MEMORISING JESUS' WORDS TO THE RICH MAN IN MARK 10.21. SEE PAGE 51 FOR TIPS ON HOW TO DO THIS.

'Go and sell all you have and give the money to the poor, and you will have riches in heaven; then come and follow me.'

 Live

Use the following diagram (taken from page 60) to help you action and live out what you have discovered in the story of the rich young man. You will see that there are hints below to help you out.

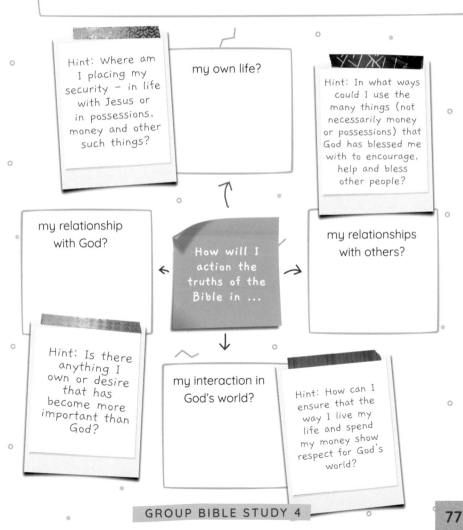

Hint: Where am I placing my security – in life with Jesus or in possessions, money and other such things?

my own life?

Hint: In what ways could I use the many things (not necessarily money or possessions) that God has blessed me with to encourage, help and bless other people?

my relationship with God?

How will I action the truths of the Bible in ...

my relationships with others?

Hint: Is there anything I own or desire that has become more important than God?

my interaction in God's world?

Hint: How can I ensure that the way I live my life and spend my money show respect for God's world?

Pray

Thank God for his words in the Bible. Ask him to show you if there is anything in your life that you have made more important than him. Commit to using your time, talents and possessions to encourage, help and bless other people.

Notes

AN EVERYDAY RHYTHM

We've put together a daily Bible reading plan with seven short personal studies (one for each day of the week), to help you get into the habit of regular Bible reading.

The plan is called 'Who am I?' It gives seven truths found in the Bible that answer this question and give us a radical new way to look at ourselves. It uses the *Inside out* Connectives throughout, and each day's reading should only take about 10–15 minutes.

Now decide when and how you are going to get stuck into the Bible using this plan. Are you a morning person or a night owl? Can you find 15 minutes when you know you won't be distracted by YouTube, Playstation or Snapchat … or fall asleep? And which day works best for you? Perhaps you have more time at the weekend, so you could find 15 minutes every Saturday and Sunday during the month. Or maybe you would prefer to do seven days in a row.

Jot down your plan of action here:

Who am I?

Sooner or later we all get around to asking ourselves the question, 'Who am I?' We want to know why we are here on the planet, why we are the way we are, and what we've got to offer to the world.

These are very important questions and it's essential that each one of us finds a satisfactory answer for ourselves. Understanding these big questions helps us become more secure, confident and happy people. We can be completely ourselves; we don't have to pretend to be someone that we're not. And who wouldn't want to be a person like that?

The Bible has some very clear answers to these questions, so each day we will look at one truth in the Bible about who we are. As you read, allow God to cement these truths into the way you think and feel about yourself – that you are someone who is loved, chosen, known, beautifully created and forgiven, with a purpose, and unique gifts and abilities.

Understanding and believing these truths about who you are as a child of God will make it less important what other people think about you and give you more freedom to be yourself.

HOW ABOUT PRINTING OUT A SELFIE IN THE MIDDLE OF A PIECE OF PAPER? STICK IT UP ON YOUR WALL AND, EACH DAY, WRITE AROUND THE PHOTO THE BIBLE VERSE OR PHRASE THAT YOU WILL BE READING. YOU COULD SCRIBBLE UP YOUR THOUGHTS AND PRAYERS AS WELL. AT THE END, YOU WILL HAVE A COMPLETE PICTURE OF 'WHO I AM'.

Pray

Ask God to help you understand what today's Bible verses could mean for you.

Read

For God loved the world so much that he gave his only Son, so that everyone who believes in him may not die but have eternal life.

JOHN 3.16

See how much the Father has loved us! His love is so great that we are called God's children – and so, in fact, we are.

1 JOHN 3.1

 Explore

Can you imagine ever loving someone else so much that you would be willing to die in their place to ensure they could continue to live? Search 'Greek words for love' on the internet: the one that's used in the Bible to describe God's love for us is *agape* (pronounced 'a-ga-pay'), and John's Gospel says that this is the biggest kind of love imaginable (John 15.13). Well, that kind of love is exactly what God has for you. He sent his Son Jesus so that you could have the best life possible, though it came at a great price – his death on the cross. God loves you so much; you are a beloved son or daughter of his. He is crazy about you!

Dig

Doodle a picture that represents you in the centre of God's love.

Question

GOD'S LOVE FOR YOU IS SOMETIMES DESCRIBED AS 'UNCONDITIONAL'. WHAT DO YOU THINK THIS MEANS?

Pray

Thank you, God, that you love me so much - more than anyone else on the planet does!

Live

When you really understand God's love for you, it doesn't matter so much what everyone else thinks about you. What difference would it make to your everyday life if you really took this to heart?

DAY 2: Someone who is chosen

 Pray

Ask God to help you understand what today's Bible verses could mean for you.

 Read

'I chose you before I gave you life, and before you were born I selected you.'

JEREMIAH 1.5

Our brothers and sisters, we know that God loves you and has chosen you to be his own.

1 THESSALONIANS 1.4

 Dig

Write out Jeremiah 1.5 or 1 Thessalonians 1.4, using a different coloured pen for each word. Think carefully about each individual word and its meaning as you write it down. Do you notice anything new?

 Explore

Have you ever been the one picked last for a sports team or group? If so, you'll know how horrible it feels to hear the groans of your team mates when they realise you're going to be on their side. Or perhaps you failed to win the art prize you worked so hard for, or didn't make it on to the team for the school technology project? Everyone knows the sinking feeling of not being chosen. Well, listen to this … God didn't groan when you made the decision to be on his side, and he hasn't left you out of his team. In fact, God chose you before you were even born. He sees your potential, and wants you right there alongside him every day.

> Now rewrite the verse in your own words.

Question

- Who were the words of Jeremiah 1.5 originally spoken to?
- What sort of job was he 'selected' for?
- Was he happy about being chosen by God?

Find out the answers to these questions by reading the first eight verses of Jeremiah chapter 1 in your own Bible.

- Who were the words of 1 Thessalonians 1.4 originally written to and from? (Look at the very first verse in the book.)
- Do you think they apply to all Christians or just a few?

Live

Jeremiah felt inadequate for the task of being a 'prophet to the nations'; he felt too young and inexperienced.

So God said to him, 'Do not say that you are too young, but go to the people I send you to, and tell them everything I command you to say. Do not be afraid of them, for I will be with you to protect you' (verses 7–8).

- In what ways do you feel inadequate or too young for God to choose you?
- What words has God given you to tell others?

Remember that God has always thought of you as valuable and that he has a purpose in mind for you. You are not too young to make a difference.

Pray

Thank God for choosing you. Tell him if you feel inadequate, nervous or unsure about his purpose for you. Spend a few minutes reflecting on Jeremiah 1.5 and 1 Thessalonians 1.4, letting the truth of God's words go deep into your heart.

Pray

Ask God to help you understand what today's Bible passage could mean for you.

DAY 3:
Someone who is Beautifully Created

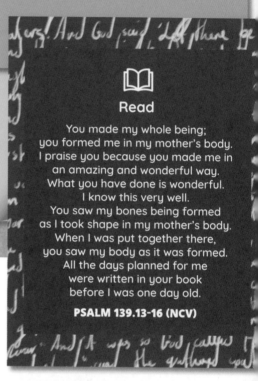

Read

You made my whole being;
you formed me in my mother's body.
I praise you because you made me in
an amazing and wonderful way.
What you have done is wonderful.
I know this very well.
You saw my bones being formed
as I took shape in my mother's body.
When I was put together there,
you saw my body as it was formed.
All the days planned for me
were written in your book
before I was one day old.

PSALM 139.13-16 (NCV)

Explore

In September 2010 Bruno Mars released a still popular single called 'Just the Way You Are'. You can find the lyrics online: they're all about how amazing the singer's girlfriend looks, just the way she is.

This single became the third biggest seller of the year and, in January 2011, it was the ninth most downloaded song of all time in the UK. There must be lots of us out there who want someone to tell us we're amazing!

Look again at the Bible passage above. The two words used to describe you in this psalm are AMAZING and WONDERFUL!

No expense was spared when God designed you and watched over you as you grew. You have been made just the way that God intended. These two words may not be the ones that you most readily use when asked to describe yourself, but in God's eyes you have been perfectly made. You are amazing and wonderful; you are exactly the way God intended you to be. So be loud and proud of who you are!

Dig

Take a selfie (no filters), or find a photo of yourself, then write or tag on the photo these words:

'I AM MADE IN AN AMAZING AND WONDERFUL WAY!'

Live

Put the photo somewhere you will regularly see it and remind yourself often that you are amazingly and wonderfully made! What difference will this make to the way you think and behave every day?

Pray

Read today's Bible passage out loud as a prayer to God, something like this:

'God, I thank you that you made my whole being. Thank you for making me in an amazing and wonderful way ...'

DAY 4: SOMEONE WHO IS FORGIVEN

Pray

Ask God to help you understand what today's Bible verses could mean for you.

Read

But if we confess our sins to God, he will keep his promise and do what is right: he will forgive us our sins and purify us from all our wrongdoing.

1 JOHN 1.9

There is no condemnation now for those who live in union with Christ Jesus.

ROMANS 8.1

Explore

Take a look at this picture. How do you think this person feels, weighed down by such a heavy load?

Being forgiven and forgiving others is a really big principle to explore in the Bible. We're all going to mess up at some time or another, whether it's letting down our parents, hurting our younger brother/sister, making a wrong decision at school or work or knowing we've displeased God in some way. The Bible calls this 'sin'. Carrying around the guilt and shame that results from our sin can make us feel just like this person. It's heavy, uncomfortable, maybe even painful. But, remember Day 1? We explored there how Jesus died for us on the cross, carrying the weight of our wrong actions for us. If we come to Jesus, we can receive complete forgiveness for our wrong thoughts and actions, and be given a clean slate to start again. Amazing! Of course, we must also forgive other people for the hurts they do to us too, just has Jesus has forgiven us.

Dig

Write or draw around the picture above anything that you wish to ask God's forgiveness for.

Pray

Pray and ask God for his forgiveness. Imagine yourself putting down the heavy load of guilt. Thank Jesus for taking it away on the cross.

Live

Put right any friendships that may have gone wrong due to unforgiveness ... today!

DAY 5: someone who has a purpose

Pray

Ask God to help you understand what today's Bible verses could mean for you.

Read

I alone know the plans I have for you, plans to bring you prosperity and not disaster, plans to bring about the future you hope for.

JEREMIAH 29.11

We know that in all things God works for good with those who love him, those whom he has called according to his purpose.

ROMANS 8.28

Explore

The verse from the book of Jeremiah is in the Old Testament part of the Bible. God spoke these words through the prophet Jeremiah to the Jews after they had been captured by an invading army and taken to Babylon, a long way from their home in Jerusalem. Look on the internet to find out exactly when this happened: try searching 'Babylonian exile'. Then explore how the story of Jeremiah fits in the overall timeline of the Old Testament. Can you find out any other interesting facts about Jeremiah's life?

The verse from the letter to the Romans is in the New Testament and was written by Paul. Christians were persecuted in Rome, so this was another difficult place for God's people to live in.

? Question

What do you think these words would have meant to God's people in Babylon and Rome?

How do these words encourage you, especially at times when it feels as if everything is going wrong?

How do you think God's purpose for you fits together with your plans for the future?

Live

You have probably been asked a hundred times what you want to do as a career. You may have already had to choose school subjects to get you on the right path towards that chosen area. It can be confusing and complicated, and you may worry that one wrong choice now might scupper all your chances in life. But these verses tell us that God will bring good out of every situation if we trust in him, and what he has got in mind for us will be way better than anything we could dream up for ourselves. So relax, follow God's lead, and walk with him into the good future that he has planned for you!

Pray

Thank you, God, that whatever situation I am in, I can take encouragement by remembering that you want the very best for me. Please help me always to ask you before making any decisions about my future, because I want your best plans for me to come true. Amen

DAY 6: SOMEONE WITH UNIQUE GIFTS AND ABILITIES

 Pray

Ask God to help you understand what today's Bible verses could mean for you.

Read

So we are to use our different gifts in accordance with the grace that God has given us. If our gift is to speak God's message, we should do it according to the faith that we have; if it is to serve, we should serve; if it is to teach, we should teach; if it is to encourage others, we should do so. Whoever shares with others should do it generously; whoever has authority should work hard; whoever shows kindness to others should do it cheerfully.

ROMANS 12.6–8

Each of you has been blessed with one of God's many wonderful gifts to be used in the service of others. So use your gift well.

1 PETER 4.10 (CEV)

Explore

Think about the main principle that you can explore in these Bible verses. Look around your friends, colleagues or classmates and you'll probably see someone who is good at art, another who excels in sport, and someone else who can do maths equations with their eyes shut. Perhaps you see someone else who is always cheerful, with a ready smile and a kind word for everyone.

We are all different, and, in line with God's plans for our lives, he has given each of us different talents and abilities. You may know already the main thing that you excel at and enjoy doing. But if you don't, that's OK. Now is the time to experience lots of different things, to discover what you feel passionate about or where you can make a difference. You see, God has given us gifts and abilities so that we can serve others, as well as give ourselves back to him. Be thankful and content with the unique you!

Question

What gifts and/or abilities do you feel God has given you? (Ask someone else what they think if you're not sure.)

 Live

Think about how you can use these gifts or abilities to help others and to serve God. Aim to do one thing to get started this week.

 Pray

Thank you, God, for my special gifts and abilities. I really want to use these gifts to help others and serve you. Please show me how. Amen

DAY 7: Someone who is known

Pray

Ask God to help you understand what today's Bible passages could mean for you.

Read

Lord, you have examined me and you know me.
You know everything I do;
from far away you understand all my thoughts.
You see me, whether I am working or resting;
you know all my actions.
Even before I speak,
you already know what I will say.
You are all round me on every side;
you protect me with your power.

PSALM 139.1–5

For only a penny you can buy two sparrows, yet not one sparrow falls to the ground without your Father's consent. As for you, even the hairs of your head have all been counted. So do not be afraid; you are worth much more than many sparrows!

MATTHEW 10.29–31

Explore

'You just don't understand!' How many times have you said that to your friends or parents? You get frustrated because they just don't seem to get what you're feeling or thinking. But God does understand. He gets you! He really does know you. He knows your thoughts, feelings and actions – good and bad. He even knows how many hairs you have on your head. Amazing!

(You may have noticed that you read some other verses from Psalm 139 on Day 3. You could read the whole psalm in your own Bible.)

Live

When you feel like no one really gets you or understands, turn to God and talk to him about it instead.

Dig

Go for a walk (or look out of the window) and notice the birds. As you walk or look around, memorise Matthew 10.29–31.

Pray

Dear God, thank you that you really know me, inside out. You know my thoughts, feelings and actions, and you understand me. Amen

Become extraordinary

Have you ever read the children's story *Once Upon an Ordinary School Day*?* In this short story an ordinary boy is pictured in his ordinary life, attending his ordinary school, expecting to be bored by his ordinary teachers. But, totally unexpectedly, into his life comes someone quite extraordinary – a new teacher called Mr Gee. Mr Gee teaches the class in a new and truly inspirational way, and something out of the ordinary happens. The children are transported to worlds beyond their wildest imagination. They see pictures of rivers and valleys and vast oceans and whales and mountains and magical things they cannot describe. They write stories of giants and heroes and villains. Their day is transformed, their imaginations run free, their perspective is blown right open … and they are inspired to dream extraordinary dreams.

We hope you have discovered that when we pick up the Bible, when we read the stories and get into God's word, things that were ordinary become extraordinary.

When we get the Bible into our lives, words that may have had no relevance become inspirational, exciting, moving, challenging and comforting. We feel like our lives have been turned inside out.

When we read the stories in the Bible of people who responded to God's invitation, we catch a glimpse of how ordinary people became extraordinary simply by living life with God.

When we read about Jesus, we realise that our ordinary lives can never be the same again. We are invited on an adventure beyond our wildest dreams.

The Bible is an extraordinary book, God is an extraordinary creator, Jesus is an extraordinary teacher, and those who live connected with the Scriptures become extraordinary too!

* *Once Upon an Ordinary School Day* by Colin McNaughton (Andersen Press, 2005)